COWBOY
PRACTICAL JOKES

By Robert M. Miller, DVM

ISBN 978-0-9834625-6-9

Published by

Robert M. Miller Communications
14415 Donnington Lane
Truckee CA 96161
www.rmmcartoons.com
email: info@robertmmiller.com

Cover and interior design by Donna Muñiz
www.silvermoongraphics.com

CONTENTS

Introduction

It's easy to understand why cowboy humor was so often expressed with practical jokes. Before I graduated veterinary school in 1956, I worked every summer as a wrangler or cowboy (wranglers work with horses, cowboys work with cattle _on_ horses). Ranch life could be very dull when once the work was completed for the day. There was no TV; on any ranch I worked on in Arizona, California, or Colorado. Going into town on Saturday night involved a drive of anywhere from 25 to 100 miles. Back then, most ranch hands didn't own an automobile.

Many bunkhouses lacked electricity so music required a hand-wound phonograph or battery radio. There was little to do in the evening except read, converse, tell jokes, play penny-ante poker, write letters, sing, or contrive practical jokes.

Pranks require ingenuity, a perverse sense of humor, and occasionally, courage. A majority of my classmates at the University Of Arizona College Of Agriculture, where I earned my pre-veterinary degree, were raised on ranches. Many were also university rodeo contestants. There were also many ranch-raised students in my Colorado vet school, and most of us were WWII veterans.
The military was also an environment conducive to practical joking.

ACKNOWLEDGEMENTS

I'm dedicating this book to my friend and colleague, Dr. Rex Hinshaw of Prescott, Arizona, because he was involved with and told me about the half-century-long practical joke described in the final chapter of this book. He shared the secret with me long ago, when we were both young. It's inspired me, although I lack what it takes to equal that supreme accomplishment.

Rex, a lifelong cowboy and cattle rancher, as well as a doctor of veterinary medicine, exemplifies the qualities it takes to be a skillful practical joker: ingenuity, brilliance, courage, persuasion, and diabolical cunning.

Thanks to Shana Jones and Kat Khree, employees at my former practice, who were somehow able to interpret my doctorate-warped handwriting and prepare this book for publication.

My thanks too, to Joe, the old cowboy who approached me one day rubbing his shoulder, and asked me for some DMSO, a medication we used for orthopedic ailments.

"What for?" I asked.

"Aah! For my old roping horse. He has a sore shoulder."

"Let me see him," I said. "A lot of times people suspect that the problem is in the shoulder when, in fact it's usually lower down the leg."

Can't," he responded. "He's up North. But I can't hurt him by rubbing DMSO on his shoulder, can I?"

"That's true" I answered. "DMSO smells bad, but the only harm it can do is shrink the testicles. But he's a gelding, so it doesn't matter."

Joe stopped rubbing his shoulder. "Well, maybe I just better try some liniment."

This incident inspired the title of a book I published in 1989 called, *Most of My Patients Are Animals*. (later reissued as, *Yes, We Treat Aardvarks*.)

Robert M. Miller, DVM

Thousand Oaks, California

Chapter 1
Growing Up

Young men like to play practical jokes, so it was inevitable that, having been to Boy Scout camp, spending a couple of years in the army, and undergoing eight years of university schooling, I was exposed to a variety of pranks. Sometimes I was a victim, sometimes a perpetrator, and often, an onlooker. Ten summers working as a cowboy taught me that no other occupation, to my knowledge, stimulates as many daring and often outrageous practical jokes as ranch work. Why?

I'm not sure, but whatever it is that motivates a person to eagerly seek a high risk, skilled career for ridiculously low wages and extreme working conditions may provide some insight.

There are two reasons for the practical joke. One is sadism and admittedly, many practical jokes are indeed sadistic, causing actual physical pain to the subject. The other is humor. As a lover of practical jokes, I much prefer the second reason.

I've been a cartoonist and a humor writer for over half a century, so I hope that humor has motivated my practical joke experiences. Certainly, I *hope* I don't possess an underlying landmine of sadism.

A predisposition to being a practical joker could be genetic but, while my parents had senses of humor, I can only recall two incidents of practical joking in which they were involved.

The first was before I was born, but my parents recounted it several times. They were at a party and a game of "Cinderella" had been initiated, wherein the victim had to go around with a lady's slipper until he found the fair maiden whose foot fit into the slipper. He would then be rewarded with a dance.

My mother sat primly on a couch, one of her legs tucked beneath her, and an artificial leg, used to display stockings in a store window, protruding from under her dress in place of her other leg.

When the victim grasped her "ankle," the leg came off. The unsuspecting dupe would then sputter, "Oh, I'm so sorry. I'm so terribly sorry."

When I was about ten years old, my folks held a birthday party for my Uncle Bill, Dad's younger brother. In

addition to a real birthday cake, my mother made one from
a square metal tray, covered with icing and candles. My
uncle was instructed to cut the cake and I spoiled the joke by
bellowing prematurely, "Feels like it's made of tin, doesn't it?"

I honestly can't remember a high school joke, but once,
as a Boy Scout, one of the older boys went into a cemetery
at night and climbed up on a monument. He was draped in a
sheet.

It was my job to lead a group of younger Scouts through
the cemetery. I still remember the eerie feeling as we made our
way through the graveyard, not knowing which statue would
start flailing its arms and screaming.

The boys, huddled behind me, were suitably frightened,
and Billy, the "statue," confessed afterward that while he
awaited for us alone in the dark, he was absolutely terrified.

Another time, at a park with stone tables overlooking a
cliff, we tied up one lad, blindfolded him, and told him we were
leaving him on a ledge at the edge of the cliff. We stifled our
laughter as the panicked young man carefully edged himself
along the table, only to feel empty space ahead of him no matter
which way he moved. Sadistic, right?

In 1945, I was sent to Camp Croft in South Carolina for infantry basic training. My platoon, comprised completely of eighteen-year-old recruits, with the exception of one 30-year-old married man we called "Pop Prescott," was quartered in a two-story barracks. My bed was on the upper floor. The showers and toilets were downstairs. We had no sooner settled into our places when one of the boys, Vincent Pinelli, stripped naked and soap and towel in hand, headed for the stairs to take a shower. As soon as he was gone, we moved his bed and belongings out of the barrack. A dozen recruits eagerly put them out on the fire escape. Then, we filled the space he'd been in with the neighboring beds and foot lockers.

We all lay reading or pretending to nap when Vincent came prancing back up to the stairs from the shower room. Naked, soap and towel in hand, he made his way to his place. It no longer existed. Nobody said anything. We all pretended not to notice him.

Finally he said, "My bed! My stuff? Where's my stuff?"

One of the lounging fellows looked at him questioningly. "What company are you in?"

"C company! Charlie!"

"Oh, that's next door. You're in the wrong barrack."

"Oh," said Vincent. "Oh!"

Then, he started to walk in circles. "But... but ..."

The poor recruit was completely confused until, finally, he spotted his footlocker outside the door to the fire escape.

There weren't too many practical jokes during the ensuing weeks of basic training. They kept us too busy, exhausted, and preoccupied with our ultimate transfer to a combat unit.

The exception was our final day at Camp Croft, when we were told that the next morning, before daylight, we were to fall out in front of the barracks with our duffel bags packed. We were to carry our rifles, bayonets, and all equipment so that we could board trucks to take us to a train headed for our next destination.

"Lights Out" in the barracks was at 9pm but by 8pm. Joe Mariner had fallen sound asleep and was snoring loudly. Our platoon leader, Sergeant Schaller, came up to see if all was well. Seeing Joe asleep he shook his shoulder and said, "Joe! Wake up! It's 5:00 A.M. and you need to be in front of the barracks in

15 minutes, ready to roll."

Joe jumped out of bed, hurriedly dressed, got all of his stuff together and went outside into the darkness. Few of the soldiers owned watches back then, so he had no way of knowing the actual time and, after all, the sergeant had ordered him out. By this time, it was Lights Out, and for the next half hour we crowded to the windows, watching poor Joe standing in the dark all alone, looking in all directions in confusion.

I preferred pranks with more imagination. For example, I made a dummy by stuffing Larry Miller's clothing (we were assigned to platoons alphabetically, so I had a Miller on each side in basic training). I put boots on the dummy, a helmet covering its "face," and stuck a bayonet through its chest. I expected Larry to be startled, and to crack up when he saw it.

Instead, Private Panko came into the barrack, saw the dummy, laughed hysterically, and then ran downstairs calling for our platoon sergeant. "Sergeant Schaller, Sargent Schaller, Private Miller committed suicide!"

A pale sergeant rushed up the stairs, saw the dummy, and growled, "Panko! You're on K.P. for a week!"

Panko protested that he hadn't created the dummy, but

our sergeant was unrelenting.

Practical jokes were also common in the army. Most showed little imagination and weren't very funny, like "short sheeting." We were required to make up our beds, to perfection, with sheets and blankets wrinkle free and pulled tight. By doubling the sheet covering the mattress, it was impossible for the victim to get all the way into bed at night. Not very funny, especially after repeat performances.

Nearly everybody smoked cigarettes back then. In my company of two hundred, there was only one non-smoker. So, in each barrack there were several large cans, half-filled with water, mounted on the walls. They were called "butt cans" and were filled with discarded cigarette butts.

An especially malicious trick was to pour the contents into a soldier's bed and then tightly cover the mess with the sheets and blankets. The object was to surprise the victim when he got into bed.

I never participated in this joke because it was done so often it had become trite, and it really inconvenienced the victim. Besides, it showed poor imagination and resulted in little laughter.

Are you a registered guest?

Chapter 2
On the Ranch

The pranks described in the previous chapter have no place in a cowboy bunkhouse. Bunkhouse humor requires ingenuity.

For example, on one summer job we moved a herd of cattle up to a U.S. Forest Service summer lease. At noon we stopped to rest, eat, and allow the herd to graze in a meadow.

As we entered the meadow, we saw a young black bear flee into the forest. After lunch our boss lay down to take a nap and put his straw hat over his face to block out the light. While he was sleeping, a forest ranger came hiking through the woods accompanied by his Boxer dog. The dog, seeing the sleeping man, went to investigate. As he snuffled and sniffed at the hat, our boss woke up, and immediately thought it was the bear. He couldn't see through the straw matting, but he felt its warm breath.

"Lie still," he thought, "Don't move."

As we watched in amusement, he rigidly pretended to be

lifeless while the dog sniffed and explored him. Then, it licked his ear. With a scream the boss exploded to his feet. He ran in one direction while the terrified dog ran the other way.

Back at the ranch a few days later we recounted the incident. It was haying time and the ranch had hired a crew to harvest. They included some vagrants and while they occupied the bunkhouse, our group of four cowboys moved into a sheep wagon nearby.

One of the haying crew was a skinny guy about 30 years of age. As we uproariously related the bear incident, he grew wide-eyed.

"Is there *bears* around here?" he asked fearfully.

Immediately sensing an opportunity, the boss said, "Oh, sure, we have plenty of bears. They kill a lot of our cattle and once in a while, we lose an employee."

For the next week, at every meal, we had bear stories to tell. The boss said, "Lost another cow last night, boys. That's the third one this week."

One of the cowboys came to dinner out of breath. "Bear nearly got me," he said, "Good thing I was on a fast horse. Chased me right up to the ranch gate."

We told the rest of the haying crew what we were up to. They found "bear tracks" all around the bunkhouse. By this time our victim was afraid to go out to the outhouse, by himself.

Finally, after a week of this, it was time to strike. Alfred was a 16-year-old "chore boy," but he was a husky kid. He draped an old buffalo hide over his head and shoulders, and stood in front of the door. We told him to just stand there, rocking from side to side.

Then, I crawled up unto the front porch. The crew sat on the floor playing cards. I rattled a trash can cover on the porch. Inside, I could see Bubba, our victim, stiffen and say, "What was that?"

The others chastised him. "Oh, play cards! Never mind the sounds outside."

After a while, I rattled the trash can cover again.

"Something's out there!" exclaimed Bubba, and through the window, I saw him stand up and listen by the door.

"Play cards!" the others insisted, and he reluctantly sat down. Once again, I rattled the cover and this time made a snarling noise.

"Something's out there!" yelled Bubba. He ran to the

door, swung it open, and there in the light coming from the open bunkhouse door was our "bear," lurching from side to side.

We expected a scream of terror and the door to be slammed shut, but instead, Bubba said, "I'll be damned." He reached behind the stove near the door, picked up a shovel, and strode out to the "bear." Those of us hiding outside yelled for Alfred to drop the buffalo robe, and Bubba lowered the shovel.

We all learned a lesson. Never underestimate another person's courage.

"What were you going to do with that shovel?" We asked afterward.

"I was gonna whomp that bear over the head," Bubba said.

In the summer of 1948, I worked on a ranch in Southern Arizona and shared a bunkhouse with a 72-yearold West Texas cowboy named Lonnie Claghorn. Lonnie told me of an elaborate joke played upon a man who got drunk in a bar in Patagonia, a cow-town east of Nogales. They hauled him out into the countryside and put him in a wagon harnessed to a horse skeleton. Then, they rigged a dummy and seated it on the wagon, holding the lines. For a head, the dummy had a cow's skull. They put red glass from a broken bottle in the eye sockets of the skull.

"What happened when he woke up?" I asked.

'Don't know!" Lonnie responded. "We just left him there and went home."

If video had existed back then, wouldn't it have been wonderful to film the passenger's waking?

A bunch of us were gathered in Prescott, Arizona's, town square one year during the annual rodeo. The square had a row of saloons known as "Whiskey Row." Most had just a bar, no tables, and no stools. You stood at the bar, had a drink, and moved on to the next place. Most of the saloons had music provided by a lone fiddler or singer/guitarist. My capacity for alcohol is limited, so after the first drink I abstained, but kept up with the rest of the rowdy crew.

An obviously drunk Bible salesman joined our group, and began mooching drinks. By the time he had followed us clear around the square and we were back in front of the Palace Hotel, Rex Hinshaw had an inspired idea. A Greyhound bus was parked in front of the hotel. Its next destination was Albuquerque. The mooching salesman had passed out.

"Let's buy him a ticket to Albuquerque," Rex suggested.

We each contributed two bucks (half a day's wages) for a one-way ticket and carried the salesman into the bus and laid him out on a bench seat in back.

I wrangled horses for the Irvine Ranch in California in 1947, and remember one of the *vaqueros* rubbing Limburger cheese into the hatband of one of his companions.

Similarly, but more malicious, the owner of a ranch I worked for one summer in Colorado invited his 30-year-old nephew to come out and help gather cattle for a branding. Jack was not a likable fellow and his boasting urban manner motivated a practical joke. *Chilitepinos* are a type of extremely hot chile pepper. One of the cowboys rubbed a handful of crushed *chilitepinos* into Jack's undershorts. Summer mornings can be cold in the Rockies, so nothing happened until late morning as we were warmed by the sun. Jack started to squirm. We all noticed and grinned and winked at each other. Then his squirming became more agitated until, finally, he bailed off his horse, frantically pulled his pants down and searched his underwear.

"What's wrong, Jack?"

"Don't know!" he bellowed, "Are there scorpions up here?"

"Do you have to pee, Jack? Why'd you pull your pants down?"

He was never told what the cause of his discomfort was, and was convinced that some sort of insect or spider had bitten him.

I wonder where George went
with that hotshot?

Chapter 3
Aggie Days

After I received my army discharge, I became a student at the University Of Arizona School Of Agriculture, with a major in Animal Husbandry. This was before I ever thought of going to veterinary school.

There were sixty of us in the class, including one woman. Most of the students were from Arizona ranches and farms. A few were from other states. Many were rodeo contestants. Inevitably, the cowboy predisposition for practical jokes manifested itself.

One day, the school rodeo club was manning a booth on campus, promoting the annual intercollegiate rodeo. I remember that Bruce Macey, Bob Prater, Dick Barney, Jake Smithers, and Ted Hazen were all there, when a reporter from the *Tucson Daily Star* showed up.

"I heard that there's a rodeo superstition about never putting your hat on a bed," he said. "Is that true?" This, is, in fact, an old superstition.

We all nodded. Under his breath, I heard the reporter

say, "Incredible! These are *college* students?"

I winked at the group and told him, "Oh, yes, we have lots of other things we believe in." I looked at Bruce and said, "Tell him about your underwear, Bruce."

"Underwear?" The reporter asked.

"Yeah, see I was wearing these undershorts and won at bull riding, so I decided I'd wear them every time because they brought me luck," Bruce explained.

"How do you know it was the underwear?" the reporter asked.

"Well, see, I normally don't wear underwear, but I did this time and I won the bull riding, so what else could it be? I've never washed them because I'm afraid the good luck will disappear, so I've been wearing them for two years now. They're kind of dirty."

The reporter took notes, his lip curled with disgust.

"Bob, tell him about your socks!"

"Okay," said Bob Prater, "Same deal. I always compete wearing the same socks and I'm afraid to wash them. I've thought about darning the holes, but I don't want to take any chances." As the gullible reporter wrote furiously, the stories got wilder and wilder, each prompting another guy to come up with a stranger story.

The *Tucson Daily Star* ran a full-page story on the weird superstitions held by college cowboys. Not one editor or the publisher realized that *they* were the dummies, not the students.

Once I thought I walked in on a practical joke, but it turned to be a real incident. The Aggie House was a fraternity house for agriculture students. A lot of my friends lived there; I resided at my parents' home in Tucson.

One summer, Jake Smithers, an Aggie House resident, and I were going up to Northern Arizona to work a roundup on the 10X Ranch, just south of the Grand Canyon. We were taking Jake's car, so my father dropped me at the Aggie House with my belongings. I was going to spend the night there so we could start the long journey before dawn the next day.

School had just ended and when I went into the house there were only two young men present, whom I didn't know. However, they were in their 20s and dressed in blue jeans and t-shirts., so I assumed that they were students.

"Hi," I said, "Is Jake here?"

"Sure," one replied. "He's upstairs." He opened the refrigerator and asked, "Do you want a beer?"

"Okay, thanks, "I said. The three of us spent the next half-hour chatting and sipping our beers.

Finally, I said, "I have to let Jake know I'm here." I excused myself and went upstairs. All of the bedrooms were empty, including Jake's.

Puzzled, I thought perhaps that he was up in the attic, which had been converted into a freshmen dormitory. As my head cleared the stairwell, I could see the entire attic. Nobody was there. Then, I heard an automobile engine roar to life.

I immediately concluded that the two strangers were troublemakers from another fraternity house, out to pull a prank. I ran down the stairs and out onto the front porch to get a glimpse of the car, but they'd vanished into the desert behind the house.

"Well," I mused, "At least I ran them off before they could do any damage."

Then, I curled up on the couch and fell asleep. A

couple of hours passed and Dick Barney arrived and he woke me up.

"What are you doing here?" he asked.

"Oh," I explained, "Jake and I are going up north in the morning to work on a ranch, so I'm spending the night here."

Dick looked around, "Where's our music center?"

"What music center?" This was before TV came to Tucson and the Aggie House had saved up money to buy a fancy record player. Obviously, I'd walked in on a couple of burglars who were raiding the unlocked frat houses while the students were out celebrating the end of the school year.

Three months later, when I got home, the Tucson police department interviewed me and asked me to describe the burglars. What could I say? They were medium-height, crew cut, in their twenties and wore jeans and t-shirts. They looked like typical college boys.

It's my own idea . . .a saddlehorn that blows!

Chapter 4
Veterinary School

In 1952, I was finally accepted into the Colorado State University School of Veterinary medicine. I continued working summers on ranches to supplement my G.I. Bill income, but it also served to increase my awareness of the cowboy propensity for practical jokes. But it was the school year itself which, despite the rigorous academic program, offered many opportunities to play pranks.

I resided, for the entire four years I studied medicine, in a barn that had been converted into student housing. The rent was $12.50 per month. We called the place the "Stud Farm." Most of the 22 residents were veterinary or pre-veterinary students. The majority were from a rural background, had cowboy experience, and several of us were rodeo contestants.

While today a majority of veterinary students are women and most come from a suburban or urban background, at the time, my school was one of the few which would accept female students. There were two women in my class- tall, strong young ladies, which was necessary in those pre-tranquilizer days. One was also a rodeo contestant.

I shared a room with two male classmates. Stan and I were from Arizona, so we occasionally received "care" packages from our families, usually containing edible treats.

Paul was from Colorado, so he got home to see his family quite often. Hence, no "care" packages. Paul had a habit of opening our packages and sampling the goodies therein. Stan and I decided to reshape his behavior.

We took a box of chocolate-covered cherries and with a hypodermic syringe aspirated the juice from several, replacing it with some habanero sauce. We left them in an accessible place, and when Paul saw them, he popped one into his mouth and bit down. Instantly, he spit out the candy and stamped on it with his foot.

Stan and I convulsed with laughter and Stan said, "Did you learn anything, Paul?" Paul replied "You guys! You just caught me by surprise! It's no problem. I *like* hot sauce."

"Well," I offered, "have another."

"Thanks, I will," and he popped another chocolate into his mouth, chewing slowly and methodically.

Paul was very blonde and light-complexioned. His face,

ears, and neck turned scarlet. Tears flowed from his eyes. He kept chewing slowly.

"Is it good?" I asked.

He nodded speechlessly.

"Have another?" I suggested.

"I would, but I don't want to spoil my dinner."

The incident unfortunately didn't stop Paul's foraging. We decided to try something else. I mentioned *chilitepinos* in a previous chapter. They're round, the size of a Spanish peanut, and red in color. I wrote home and asked my father to send me some *chilitepinos*. When they arrived, I mixed them with some Spanish peanuts and left them in a bowl on my desk. Paul came in while I was studying, said, "Ah! Peanuts!" grabbed a handful, and stuffed them in his mouth. That did the trick.

Chilitepinos are incredibly hot. I took the bowl of mixed peppers and peanuts to school with me the next day, planning some sort of prank, but as I entered the anatomy lab I passed Lyman White who bellowed, "Ah! Peanuts!" He grabbed a handful and tossed them in his mouth. Lyman was six-and-a-half feet tall, and a rodeo star. I fled in one direction while he fled in the opposite direction, toward the water fountain.

Bob Schild wasn't a classmate while I was in veterinary school, but he attended the university at the same time as I did, majoring in agriculture. An Idaho ranch kid, he was a great rodeo bronc rider. Bob worked in the school cafeteria between classes to help pay for his education. There were cliques in the cafeteria: vet students at one table, forestry majors at another, and so on. The rodeo contestant table was always popular. Because I was a cartoonist, Bob asked me to caricature his friends at the rodeo table, and to make the cartoons as offensive as possible. This I did, and Bob would post them in the cafeteria, inside the bookstore window so they couldn't be removed. He would then enjoy the outrage displayed by the rodeo crew. This went on for a long time. My life was in jeopardy, but Bob never revealed the identity of the cartoonist. The entire thing became a regular subject in the campus newspaper, which sponsored a witch hunt for the cartooning culprit, with Bob Schild vociferously vowing to personally destroy him if his identity became known.

Before I started vet school, I worked for a veterinarian in Tucson. During a visit home I called the doctor, and affecting a Southern accent, I said "Mah boll weevils are dyin'. Can you help me?" He said "Sorry, I'm not an entomologist. Why don't you call an entomologist at the University of Arizona?"

"I did," I explained "An' he said he knew all about healthy weevils, but if they're dyin' I should call a vet."

His curiosity apparently aroused, he asked "Why are you concerned? All the cotton farmers want the boll weevils to die."

"Well" I said "You know how some people keep ant farms as a hobby?"

"Yes"

"An' you know some people raise bees for a hobby?"

"Yes"

"Well, ah raise boll weevils. Ah'm from Texas an ah guess it reminds me of home"

"I'm sorry," the vet said impatiently. "I can't help you."

"Wait a minute," I quickly replied. "Ah have another problem. Ah have to go out of town an ah need a place to board my weevils. Can you do that for me?"

"Gosh, I've never been asked to do that before," my former employer said. "What do you feed them?"

"Why *cotton* of course, you damn fool!" I roared.

There was a long silence. Then he asked "Miller, is that you?"

I tell this story to illustrate the fact that it's easy to pull practical jokes on veterinarians. The profession meets with so many unusual situations that they accept the most bizarre stories as real.

For example, before I began vet school, I worked for a veterinarian in Tucson. Once, when the circus was in town I phoned him pretending to be an elephant trainer. I told him that I had a constipated elephant that needed an enema.

I expected a shocked reaction but instead, Doctor Shannon blithely answered, "Okay, I'll be out after my office closes, at 6pm."

Later in my career, I was actually called to see constipated elephants more than once at our local zoo.

Yeah, I know, but she gives us a good
calf every year. Let's run her again.

Chapter 5
1954, "The Year of the Joke" Begins

I didn't experience this practical joke but it was told to me, and I repeat it here to illustrate the complexity and ingenuity within the cowboy culture of practical jokes.

I worked one summer for the UT Bar Ranch in Colorado and this story was told to me by the owner of the adjacent McCarthy Ranch. He had a cowboy we'll call Bill, who resided in a bunkhouse served by an outhouse. To celebrate Halloween Bill decided to drag the privy out into the middle of the Laramie River, which ran through both of the aforementioned ranches. Needing assistance, he asked Ken, a neighboring UT Bar cowboy to help him.

The plan was to ride out at night on two good roping horses, rope the privy, and drag it out to a sandbar in the middle of the Laramie River. What amused them was the consternation that would occur the next morning when ranch personnel discovered their privy in the middle of the river, which averaged about three or four feet in depth.

Ken mentioned the plan to his boss, Rick, who came up

with a better idea. He convinced Ken to cooperate, backfiring the joke on Bill in a way which might effectively discourage him from ever again trying to commit a practical joke on anyone.

Rick told Mr. McCarthy what Bill was planning to do. Then they hatched the counter-attack.

On Halloween night, Bill and Ken roped the privy as planned and started to drag it. Suddenly they heard shotgun blasts and McCarthy shouting that he'd kill the invaders.

Both cowboys ran away from the gunfire at top speed, Ken crying out,
"I'm shot! I'm shot!" and leaning forward in the saddle. After they crossed the river they ran their horses all the way back to the UT Bar. There, while Ken slumped in the saddle, Bill cried out for help.

Rick came out of the ranch house and helped Ken out of the saddle. He opened Ken's jacket. Under his shirt Ken had a thin bloody flank steak.

As Rick opened Ken's shirt, exposing bloody flesh, Bill cried out in horror. It was all his fault. His friend had been shot, possibly fatally, because of his fool stunt.

Rick had John carry the now "unconscious" Ken to a

bedroom where Rick and his wife prepared to help the dying man. They chased Bill out of the room.

After a suitable length of time allowing Bill to grieve and berate himself, Ken walked out of the bedroom and said, "Hi, Bill!"

This story illustrates just how far cowboy humor can carry a practical joke, especially in the past when there was little in the way of entertainment to occupy free time in the bunkhouse.

In 1954, during a summer job on a Northern Colorado ranch near the Wyoming border, what I still call "The Year of the Joke" began.

A television company decided to make an agricultural documentary program called "Beef." It was to be the journey of a calf, from its birth on the ranch to the dinner table.

The ranch scenes were to be filmed on the ranch I worked for, starting with the calving and followed by the spring round-up and branding. The host and narrator for the show was a young man who had started his career in radio and was later to become one of TV's most recognizable news program anchors:: Hugh Downs.

Hugh arrived at the ranch two weeks before the scheduled filming and accompanied us on a cattle drive. He was an experienced rider, which is but one of his many talents. I learned that Hugh Downs was a20th century Renaissance Man," and that summer began a lifelong friendship between us.

Hugh is an experienced scuba diver, a licensed balloon, glider, and airplane pilot, an author, a historian, authority on firearms, teacher and lecturer. He's conducted symphony orchestras and has been all over the world. But what may be his foremost talent was his ability to conceive practical jokes. For example, he told me of a radio announcer whom they repeatedly tried to crack up when he was doing commercials. The announcer was apparently immune to every effort.

However, his self-control met its match one day when Hugh, in the control booth, confronted the announcer with a hot dog protruding from the fly of his pants.

When the announcer looked up, Hugh snipped the hot dog in two with a pair of large shears. That did it! The announcer broke up. Obviously, practical joking isn't limited to cowboys.

Hugh told us this story as part of a discussion about practical jokes, because he was planning one and needed our cooperation.

The TV show's producer, Clint Youle, was going to join us

when filming was ready to commence, along with his wife, two daughters, and the other crew members. They planned to fly from New York to Denver, and then take a small private plane to the airstrip on a ranch bordering the one we were at.

Hugh decided to have the group picked up with a wagon drawn by a team of horses and then, on the way to our ranch, have me and another cowboy, 19-year-old Bob Crist, ride up with masks on and stage a holdup. He asked our boss, the owner of the ranch, if he'd be amenable and the plan was presented to me and Crist. We discussed it and came up with what we thought was a better plan.

I spoke to Hugh, telling him Mr. Youle couldn't possibly be naïve enough to fall for such an obviously staged hold-up. I suggested that they pick up the family as planned, but to leave the robbery to us. All the crew on the wagon had to do is pretend that they had never seen us before.

Bob Crist and I quit shaving for a week. Then, on the day the airplane landed on the neighboring ranch, the Youle family was picked up with a team and wagon accompanied by Hugh, the ranch owners, and another cowboy driving the team. This, of course, was a pleasant surprise to these urban Easterners.

As they drove back to our ranch headquarters, Bob Crist and I came riding up the trail. The TV cameraman, Marshall Head, asked if the two riders were "a couple of your boys?" Our boss answered, "Yes, I think so."

The cowboy driving said, "I don't think so. They look like a couple of saddle tramps to me."

This is what set the stage for what followed.

Marshall Head immediately started filming with his camera to record the colorful scene.

Besides not shaving for a week, Bob and I had smeared mud over our horse's brands, had bed rolls tied behind our saddles, carried rifles in scabbards, and wore soiled clothes. Bob also had a revolver hidden in his chaps' pocket. At my request, the people on the wagon who were in on the joke had empty wallets.

As we approached the wagon, I cheerfully called out "Howdy!" My companion, meanwhile, maintained a grim and unsmiling expression.

"Did I see an airplane land up yonder?" I asked.

"Yes," said the boss. "We're picking up this family from back East. They're going to stay with us a while."

"Well, I'll be damned," I drawled. "Are there any deer in

the mountains up ahead?"

"Yes" said my boss. "But it's not deer hunting season."

"That doesn't bother us none." I grinned.

Our character had now been established.

"Well, you boys be careful. We have to get these folks home." He clucked at the horses and started to move off.

"Wait a second!" I called. The wagon stopped.

"I got an idea! You folks look prosperous, and me and my partner are hard up. Why don't you all put your wallets in a hat and give them to me."

This brought a chorus of protests from the wagon and my boss warned, "That's not funny, son."

"I'm not trying to be funny," I said. "We need the money and don't get my partner mad, because he has a terrible temper."

All eyes now turned towards Bob, who sat several yards away with his revolver positioned across his saddle horn, pointing at the wagon.

There were gasps, and I softened at the frightened expression on the mother's and daughters' faces.

Our boss climbed down from the wagon, his hat filled with wallets. "You boys are making a big mistake," he said. "It's not too late to back off."

My smile disappeared and I growled, "You mind your own damn business and do as you're told." He smiled and bit his lip, but his back was to the wagon and the passengers couldn't see his face.

I transferred the wallets to my saddlebag and both of us whirled and rode away, hooting and yelping, at top speed.

"Don't look back at us!" I shouted, but cameraman Marshall whipped up his camera and filmed us as we rode away. "I got them on film!" he yelled, victorious.

Bob and I rested our horses and gloated over our success. Then, after waiting long enough for the wagon to reach ranch headquarters, we headed that way, assuming that by now the joke was revealed and everybody was laughing.

But that isn't what happened. As soon as they arrived, Mr. Youle took over. He insisted on calling the police. The sheriff in Laramie was already prepared for the call because he was in on the joke. So he explained to Mr. Youle that we were 80 miles away from Laramie, the closest law enforcement, and that they probably couldn't have anybody arrive in less than two hours.

Mr. Youle noticed that a variety of rifles and shotguns were hung on the ranch office wall.

"Listen," he said. "Those men will be up in the mountains before the sheriff gets here. Let's load these guns and go after them."

He was serious. Like Bubba and the bear, you never know how a man will react to an emergency situation. Mr. Youle said, "Your station wagon can make it up that trail, let's go after them."

The ranch staff protested, insisting that by now the robbers would be long gone, and besides, they looked crazy enough to be really dangerous. Then they decided to tell the truth.

Youle didn't believe them. He thought staff was trying to protect him. He insisted, "Look, I'm sure a car can get up that trail. You don't need a horse and wagon." He was right, of course. Vehicles used the trail all the time.

"They'll get away if we don't go after them right now." Then he demanded ammunition for the rifles.

At this point, our boss jumped into a station wagon and tore up the hill, knowing that we were on our way down. He flagged us down, explained the situation, and told us to stay put until we were told it was safe.

When we finally got down to the ranch, Mrs. Youle, with

tears in her eyes, shook her finger at us disapprovingly. Mr. Youle was laughing, but relieved, and Marshall Head was disappointed because he hadn't filmed a real holdup.

The story of the fake holdup made the *Denver Post,* and, I was told, some other newspapers.

The experience whetted our appetite for practical jokes, and some diabolical plots were conceived and finally implemented after the film crew left the ranch.

For example, the ranch had an old homestead that had obviously failed, and the owners had sold out their land to the ranch surrounding it. The cabin, disintegrating from neglect, still had its furnishings and even some canned food in the pantry.

There wasn't much to do in the evenings in those pre-television days. You could read, play cards, or tell jokes. One night the boss, who was also a practical joker, asked one of the cowboys to go check a gate that had been left open. The cowboy went to the door and said, "Anybody want to go with me?"

There were three guests in the room enjoying the fireplace, but they all immediately said, "Sure". They got into the station wagon and, with the cowboy driving, went to the cabin.

As expected, the passenger said "Who lives there? What's

the cabin for?"

"Oh, a homesteading couple lived there once, but she was murdered. Terribly mutilated. And her husband disappeared. The people around here are superstitious and say the place is haunted. I'll just close the gate."

"Wait! Can we drive down to see the place?"

"Well," the driver hesitated. "It's kind of dark."

The guests laughed. "Are you afraid?"

"No. I'll drive closer, and you can go in the house if you want to. But I'm not going in."

Slowly, the cowboy drove towards the little home. The front door was open, and the headlights shined illuminated the driveway.

I was hiding behind the door, wearing an ankle-length yellow slicker. I had a nylon stocking pulled over my head to make my features grotesque, and an old, worn Stetson top of my head.

I stepped out from behind the door, unable to see because of the headlights., I felt my way one foot at a time, through the door and down the stairs towards the headlights.

The screaming in the car was unbelievable, and the vehicle

rocked back and forth. The driver pretended it wouldn't start. Slowly, I came closer. Finally, the engine caught and the car screeched into reverse, whipped around, and tore up the hill.

I removed the stocking, went to my own car, which I'd hidden behind the house, drove back to the ranch house, snuck in through a back door, and pulled the stocking back over my head.

I could hear the boss's voice as I made my way to the room, which was illuminated only by the fireplace.

"No wonder the people around here say that place is haunted."

Then, one of the guests-an older educated man who worked as an engineer- said, "There has to be a logical explanation for this. We didn't see a ghost. That's impossible. Maybe some vagrant has moved in there."

"But," another guest protested, "It had no legs! No feet! Just a head and a horrible face and a body. It floated out the door. It couldn't be a live human being."

At this point, blinded by the stocking over my face, I cautiously felt my way towards the fireplace. Then somebody saw me. There was a terrified scream, and another, and then, everybody was convulsing with laughter.

Two weeks later a honeymooning couple stayed at the ranch. We pulled the same routine, except that this time we let them come into the house with a flashlight.

I dressed the same way, but this time I got into the bed and covered myself completely with a filthy, moldy old quilt. The cowboy driver declined to enter the house, but the young honeymooners did, using a flashlight. When they entered the room where I was hiding under the quilt, the bride gasped, "Oh! That scared me! It looks just like someone's in the bed."

I waited a few seconds, and then slowly sat up.

The bride, holding the flashlight, rocketed through the door. The groom, unable to see, ran into the plasterboard wall, punching a huge hole in it.

Another time, we did it again. This time I drove the station wagon, and two of the other ranch employees hid outside, behind the house. One sat on the other's shoulders, creating a monster over eight-feet-high. But this time we went too far. As the apparition came out from behind the house into the headlights, our intended victim said, "Oh, come on! You guys must think I'm stupid."

"Mounted Police, M'am!"

Chapter 6
"The Year of the Joke" Continues

I returned to school in the fall of 1954, my appetite for practical jokes whetted. Most of the 22 residents at the "Stud Farm" were the same guys as had lived there the previous year. Some, including me and my two roommates, were in the lower floor of what had once been a barn. A few more roomed above, in what had once been the hayloft. One occupied the former chicken coop. The rest of the students lived in the basement of the landlord's house. One of them was a freshman pre-veterinary student from New Jersey. His name was John.

The only building more than two stories tall in Fort Collins, Colorado, in 1954 was the Great Northern Hotel. Every Sunday night its restaurant featured, for 98 cents, a lavish, all-you-can-eat Italian dinner. There were white tablecloths and candles, and three excellent entrees: spaghetti, lasagna, and ravioli. Drinking water and coffee were included.

So every Sunday evening, a group of us from the barn would go to the Great Northern Hotel to stuff ourselves, and afterwards go to the nearby theatre to see a double feature movie for 45cents.

I was one of the few students who owned a car. It was a derelict Plymouth I had purchased when I worked in Denver the year before I was accepted into veterinary school.

As six of us trooped out to my car, John said "Hi guys! Where are you going?"

Immediately one of the students answered matter-of-factly, "To a whorehouse in Laramie. We go every Sunday night."

Laramie, Wyoming, was an hour's drive from Fort Collins, Colorado. It was the home of the University of Wyoming and, in 1954, it also had a notorious red light district with prostitutes no student could possibly afford.

After the movie that night, we drove back to the "Stud Farm" and I went to bed. I was fast asleep when, around midnight, I awoke with a start. John was standing next to my bunk, shining a flashlight in my face.

"Sorry" he said. "I thought you might still be awake, You know, you're one of the older guys in this place, a war veteran, and a third-year vet student, so I look up to you. That's why I was surprised by what you guys did tonight."

Then he opened a Bible and started to read passages to me:

"Thou shalt not commit adultery," and so on. "How do I handle this?" I thought. Should I just tell him we were kidding, and that we just went to dinner and a movie?

No! This was a great opportunity.

I told him that this wasn't an ordinary whorehouse. It was a farmhouse, and all of the girls there were students at the University of Wyoming. None of them could afford to go to college. All were from poor families, or orphans. But they all had high goals, to become educated, productive members of society. Moreover, no customers were allowed into the farmhouse unless they too were college students. Most were from the local university, while others, like us, were from Fort Collins, the University of Colorado, or Denver University. I explained that no one was allowed to enter the house unless they could showed a current college matriculation card. Then I mentioned how low the prices were at the "Farmhouse" because-after all-we were students.

The next day I told everybody in the house about our conversation, and pledged them to silence.

On Wednesday John came to my room and asked if we were going to Laramie again on Sunday. I said "Of course! We wait all week for those wonderful few hours with those beautiful girls."

"Listen," he said. "I'd like to go with you. Now, I'm only going to observe. I'm not going to do anything sinful."

"No problem," I reassured him. "We'll welcome your company."

We all conspired for the next few days and planned our actions.

Sunday, at 6pm, John appeared, decked out in new cowboy boots and a western hat.

"When are you going to Laramie?" he asked.

"In a few minutes," we assured him.

This time we needed three cars to hold all the conspirators. John grinned as we told him, "You're not going to be able to resist these girls. And the first time you go to bed with one of them, it's free."

When we pulled up at the Great Northern Hotel, John said, "Why are we here?"

"We always eat first," said Mike.

"We'll need our strength in Laramie," added Richard.

"I wish I'd known." said John. "I already had my dinner, but I'll just keep you company."

As we ate, the conversation was all positive. We expressed our anticipation for the evening ahead. We raved about the girls. Then Ed said, "Hey, you know who would be perfect for John? *Nancy!*"

"Oh, yes," we all agreed. "She's perfect. They're both eighteen, the same age. And she's petite, just the right size for John."

"And she adores virgins!"

John's eyes sparkled, and he giggled helplessly.

Then, halfway through dinner, the conversation abruptly changed, according to our carefully planned script.

"Say," said Ed. "Isn't it a shame what happened to that Forestry student in Laramie?"

"Yeah," said Walter. "The cop wouldn't have shot him if he hadn't protested the arrest; he should have surrendered quietly."

"Damn shame," said Ed. "That's the third guy the cops hurt this year. Remember that Chemistry major the cops beat up so badly last month?"

"Yeah, and the Denver U guy who tried to run from the house without his pants on?"

We could all see John stiffen and frown.

Mike changed the subject. "Hey, let's think of positive things. You know who cracks me up every Sunday? It's Louise! It's not because she's so fat and has a mustache. It's because she's so funny!"

"Yeah, and those missing teeth make it even funnier!"

John lurched to his feet and bellowed, "I thank the Lord for letting me see the light before it was too late!" before he stormed out of the restaurant.

He walked the half-mile from the town center to the "Stud Farm" while we finished our meal and then went to the movies.

After we returned, three of us went to John's room in the basement. He was awake reading.

"John," we said. "Why did you leave us? What did we say to offend you?"

"I've been saved!" he shouted. "In the nick of time. You guys and your farmhouse! What about the cops shooting students and what about Louise? She doesn't sound like a fairytale student."

"She's *not*!" we reassured him. "She's the *maid* at the farmhouse."

"Yeah? What about the cops shooting those guys?"

"That wasn't at the farmhouse. That was in the red light district. Things like that don't happen at the farmhouse."

"Oh," said John. "I misunderstood."

By the next Sunday John was eager to go with us again. But this time we had a new tactic. We explained to him, "John, we feel guilty trying to get you to do what we all know is immoral. So we can't take you with us."

"But," he protested. "All I want to do is observe!"

"John," I said patiently. "There's no way that you'll be able to resist those gorgeous girls. We can't be responsible for ruining a chaste man's life. You can't go with us."

That's the way things went for several weeks. Then we got a new idea.

Gene Taylor, one of the veterinary students at the Stud Farm, had a girlfriend at the University of Wyoming who eventually became his wife. He made frequent trips to Laramie to see Alice.

We had Alice, in her feminine script, write a letter to John. In it she explained that she was known as Nancy at the farmhouse, but her real name was Wanda. She pledged him not to reveal that. She said that she knew the other students in our group teased him and were provocative. She said that she greatly admired him for his pure values and begged him not to come up the farmhouse because she knew that the girls, herself included, would find him an irresistible challenge. She explained that she could only love a man with such a noble character, and she didn't want him spoiled. Finally, she asked for a picture of him.

There was no return address, so on Sunday John gave us a sealed envelope before we left for dinner, and asked that we give it to Nancy that evening. At the dinner table we passed the letter around gleefully, planning our next move.

Thus began an exchange of letters. Nancy (Wanda) thought he was very "cute". Again, she praised his virginity and enclosed a photo of herself. (One of the guys had a picture of his high school homecoming queen)

In a few weeks, John was hopelessly in love with Nancy (Wanda). He begged for her return address and full name so he didn't have to have us deliver his letters when we went to Laramie on Sunday nights. We declined to "protect" him.

Nancy (Wanda) finally admitted that she was in love with John. He responded, admitting that he had fallen in love with her and longed to meet. She declined, expressing concern that she would feel guilty because she knew she'd end up in bed with him.

Months passed while this exchange of letters went on.

Finally, he proposed marriage. He said he couldn't live without her, and confessed to masturbating nightly. He explained that she had caused him to sin, and that by marrying they would both sin no more.

We knew we'd gone too far. We knew that we had to disillusion him so that he'd give up loving Nancy (Wanda). We also knew that it had to be his idea. We didn't dare let him know that he was the victim of an elaborate practical joke.

Our landlord got involved in our plot. One evening as John returned from the school library, our landlord met him.

"John," he said. "There's been somebody here all afternoon waiting to see you. She was so disappointed she had to get back to Laramie.." John was stunned.

The landlord asked curiously, "Who is this girl, John? How do you know her? She's sure beautiful."

"Oh," John explained. She's just somebody I know. Did she say she's coming back?"

"No, but she seemed very disappointed. Gosh, she's sure gorgeous."

One day, John got on a bus and went to Laramie. He made his way to the red light district and asked people there if they knew of a whorehouse called "The Farmhouse." None did.

He asked scores of people if they knew a beautiful girl named Nancy. He found one that did.

Is she petite and gorgeous?" he asked.

"You bet!"

"Is she a student at the University?"

"Could be!"

But, his day was wasted and we knew that we had to bring this thing to a graceful end.

I had dated a girl on campus from a prominent Colorado family. Profanity, so commonly used by young women today, was a rarity in 1954. This girl, an attractive blond, was proud of her nickname, "Garbage Mouth." She enjoyed shocking people.

I recruited her for our mission. After hearing the details, she was eager to assist. So a group of us went to her sorority house and gathered around a telephone in the parlor. She called John.

There was only one telephone at the "Stud Farm." It was a pay phone on the porch.

"Garbage Mouth" got John on the phone and said "It's me!

Wanda!"

We all gathered around the phone to listen.

"Wanda!" he shouted. "Nancy! Wanda! Where are you?"

"I'm here in Laramie. I'm at a party. I wish you were here." She slurred her speech and said "Give me another shot of that booze."

"You're *drinking*?" he asked. "I thought you didn't drink. You told me that!"

"Don't be a dumbshit," she said.

Meanwhile, trying to stifle our laughter, our group of pranksters gathered around the telephone and said things like "Come on, babe! Get off the phone before you're too drunk to screw all of us!" and "I get to lay her first. It's my turn."

Then, Garbage Mouth said, "Hey, you son of a bitch, get your hands out from under my skirt. You can't do that until I give you permission."

There was a long silence. Then, John said, "I thank the Lord I was saved before I made a terrible mistake."

He hung up the telephone, and that was the end of the John/ Great Northern Hotel/Laramie Affair.

John didn't return to our school the next year. But a close

friend of his, a pre-veterinary student named Gordon did. He told us that John had decided on a military career and was now attending a military school. Then, he said he wanted to ask us a question.

"John was corresponding with a girl in Laramie," he said.

"He told me that you and the other vet students here knew her. I'd like to get in touch with her. Can you help me?"

All I know," I replied, "is that her name was Nancy. I'm a senior and getting ready to take State Board exams in order to get licenses to practice, so I can't be going up to Laramie on Sundays. I'll be swamped with clinic duty, senior courses, and getting ready for exams."

Then, I gathered the "Stud Farm" gang and told them we had another sucker if they wanted to do the whole year-long routine again.

However, the novelty had worn off and we all declined to get involved again. My senior year was devoid of practical jokes.

Thirty-three years later, Gordon was a doctor of veterinary medicine practicing in the same county as me. One evening, at a county veterinary association meeting, I found myself sitting next to him at the dinner table.

"Do you ever get back to Fort Collins?" he asked.

"Yes, once in a while. I've lectured at the school and been to some other events there."

It's changed a lot," he said. "It's a much bigger university and, of course, it's not called Colorado A&M anymore

"Right!" I agreed. It's Colorado State University now."

"Yes," he said.

Gordon was a quiet, reserved man.

"Do you remember...oh, I suppose you don't. It's been so long."

"What?" I asked.

"Do you remember a classmate of mine? His name was John."

"Sure! He was a pre-vet from New Jersey."

"Wow! You have a great memory. Do you remember...? I'm sure you don't, but there was a girl, in Laramie, a student at the University there he was corresponding with. Oh, I'm sure you were too busy in vet school to remember."

"But, I do!" I said. "Her name was Nancy, but not really. Her real name was Wanda."

Gordon stared at me. "Wow! You do have a good memory.

Yes!"

Then, after a pause, he asked, "What was that all about?"

"It was all a practical joke," I explained. "There was no such person. It was a joke."

Gordon looked perplexed.

"But I saw her letters. John showed me all her letters."

"We wrote the letters," I explained.

"It was all a practical joke. We wrote the letters and Gene Taylor took them up to Laramie. His fiancée, Alice, re-wrote them and mailed them to John at the place we lived. Then he gave his answering letters to Gene, because he didn't know her address in Laramie, so Gene could deliver them to her. But then we'd open the letters and all crack up laughing. It went on for most of the school year until John broke it off himself. He never found out, and we never told him. It was all an elaborate practical joke."

Gordon stared into space. He'd stopped eating. His only response was a long, drawn-out, "Ooooooooh." Understanding, at long last, dawned on his face.

In early 2013 the news broadcasts were preoccupied with the story of a Notre Dame University football star, Manti Te'o, a very likeable and decent young man from Hawaii. He was in love with a girl he'd never met, Lennay Kekua. The relationship had been exclusively online and Kakua had been presented as a beautiful, religious, family-oriented girl with a Polynesian background. Then, Lennay died of leukemia. News outlets told the tragic story, and then Manti learned that it was all a hoax. Lennay had never existed. Notre Dame's Athletic Director, Jack Swarbrick, called it a "sophisticated hoax perpetuated for reasons we can't fully understand." *I* understand! Many said it wasn't possible for a college student to be so deceived. Oh yes, it's possible. I *know* how possible it is.

Hey, Coosie, sorry to hear about us losin' that mule yesterday!

Chapter 7
"The Year of the Joke" Continues

An entire school year is a long time for a practical joke to continue, but John's romance with Nancy wasn't the only one the residents of the "Stud Farm" pulled in 1955. There was another one, just as involved, just as ingenious, and just as entertaining to a bunch of college students who had never seen television.

Lash was a pre-veterinary student. We called him Lash because he owned a bullwhip and was fond of cracking it. A popular motion picture Western hero of the day was an actor named Lash LaRue. Rather than using six-guns, he used a bullwhip and therefore, our fellow "Stud Farm" resident was nicknamed Lash the first day of school.

When classes started, Lash had attended a demonstration in hypnotism put on by one of the professors who routinely did this on the first day of class for the students in her introductory psychology class. She used student volunteers for her demonstration and was said to be very effective.

Lash was intrigued and confident that he could do the same thing. So that night he asked his roommate if he was willing to be a subject for hypnotism.

The roommate agreed and while stretched out on his bed, Lash began the hypnotic ritual as he had watched his teacher do it.

The roommate, Fred, a kid from a tiny ranching community in the heart of the Colorado Rockies pretended to be hypnotized, even allowing Lash to poke him with a pin after the would-be hypnotist had told his subject, "You will feel no pain."

Lash was so excited by his success that he invited a group of us from the "Stud Farm" to observe his skill. Fred, meanwhile, had warned us that he was faking a trance.

After seeing his skill as a hypnotist, every other student in the house volunteered to be hypnotized. We all faked it but Lash was so thrilled by his talent that he decided to change his major from pre-veterinary to psychology.

At this time there was considerable global interest in what was called the "Bridie Murphy" affair. A hypnotist had revealed a previous life in a subject who had, centuries earlier, been an Irish housemaid named Bridie Murphy. Many people were convinced that this was evidence of reincarnation. Of course, the whole thing was eventually proved to be nonsense, but at the time many in academia were intrigued.

After many "hypnotism" sessions, we all got tired of being stabbed with pins. So one evening when Lash offered to hypnotize his roommate, Fred suggested that Lash take him back in time to see if they could duplicate the Bridie Murphy experiment.

Lash didn't know that Fred's grandfather had been a Civil War captain. So, when Fred was in his "trance" and Lash took him back a decade at a time, when he got to the year 1863, Fred responded. He mumbled, mentioned names and places, and a battle.

Lash ran to the library and confirmed that the incidents had really occurred.

He knew that Duke University was conducting its own study into the Bridie Murphy business and wanted them to know that he had obtained a similar result. Duke University got excited, encouraged Lash to go on with his efforts, and sent him a wire recorder so he could record his hypnotic sessions.

Lash asked us if we were willing to become subjects for his study. Of course, we agreed. We had all been successfully "hypnotized" by Lash, some of us several times. Lash had now purchased a turban to wear while he was hypnotizing and had put a blue light bulb in his basement room.

The first person he did was Gene Taylor. He took Gene back to the 1840's when Gene stirred and mumbled. Lash asked, "Who are you? Where are you?"

Gene's response was, "Don't beat me no mo', massa! I be good. I pick cotton. Jus' don't beat me no mo'!"

Gene, in a former life had been a slave in Georgia.

Next he did Gene Kalisz. What Lash didn't know was that Kalisz, as a boy scout, had been to a camp in Idaho, a former home of a lesser- known Indian tribe called the Sheepeaters. When "hypnotized" and taken back in time, he turned into a Sheepeater. He chanted and drummed very authentically and Lash recorded all this.

Lash had no way of knowing that when I was a boy, I was fascinated by stories of the old New England whaling industry. I know ship names and the terminology of the whalers. So when he hypnotized me and took me back in time I became the first mate on a New Bedford whaler. I arose in a trance, picked up a ski pole, got on top of a dresser, yelled, "Thar She Blows" and threw the ski pole like a harpoon.

Each of us came up with increasingly complex previous lives, each trying to outdo those who had been done before. Lash sent his results to an excited Duke University.

It was Walter Cole's turn. He told me, "Tell Lash to take me way back, thousands of years."

So Lash induced Walter, who lay on Stan Teeter's cot in our room in the barn. He seemed to be in a deep trance. Lash took him back all the way to 1600 A.D. with no response. I suggested he go back by the centuries rather than decades. He did so.

"It's the fourth century, Do you remember anything?"

No response.

When he reached 1000 B.C. I suggested he try going by millennia. Lash complied and by 20,000 B.C. he was ready to give up. I urged him to keep trying. Finally, at 24,000 B.C. Walter stirred.

Do you remember anything?

Walter groaned.

"What do you remember?"

Now Walter opened his eyes. On the wall over Stan's bed was a picture of a skeleton of a horse. (We were veterinary students)

Walter grunted, smiled, sat up, and stroked the picture. Then he turned, looked at us, grabbed a hammer on a table next to the bed, and dove under the bed. Threatening us with the hammer he snarled and growled.

Lash clapped his hands and ordered, "Wake up! I order you to wake up! When I say three! One, two, three! Wake up!"

It was no use. Walter stayed under the bed, growling and waving the hammer until Lash decided to give up, leave him in the room, the lights out, and the door locked.

The school year was half over, Duke University was being sucked into a college prank, and we were afraid that we would get into trouble or possibly, expelled. So I volunteered to go to the head of the psychology department and tell her the truth. I did so and she said that she had heard all about it from Duke University and had suspected a college prank. She suggested we terminate it but to do so without damaging Lash.

In other words, just like the love affair with John and Nancy, quitting had to be his idea.

We worked out a plan. First Fred went into a trance at the dinner table and started giving orders to a Civil War artillery battery. We all pretended to be stunned and Lash said, "I know what's wrong! Let me handle it! Fred, wake up!"

No response.

Fred said "Fire One!"

Lash said, "I command you to wake up."

"Fire two!"

"Wake up!"

"Fire three!"

Finally, Lash said, "I'll never hypnotize *him* again!"

Exactly the response we wanted.

Following this, each day someone went into a hypnotic trance and did ridiculous things.

For example, one afternoon I went to Lash's room and told him that I had an important final exam the next day, but I was having trouble studying. I asked if he could put me into a hypnotic trance and suggest that I be relaxed and memorize whatever I read that evening. He put on his turban, turned on the blue light and quickly put me into a trance and then intoned "Whatever you study today, you will never forget. You will be relaxed and confident. When you go to class tomorrow you will_"

At this point I rose, robot-like, and walked out of the room. Lash ran after me saying, "I didn't tell you to get up! Stop! Wake up! I command you to wake up!"

Ignoring him, I walked outside like a robot, got into my old car, started the engine and put the transmission into reverse. Lash kept shouting "Wake up! Bob! I command you! One, two, three!"

I drove down the street backward, Lash running alongside, I turned the corner off of Meldrum Street and kept driving backward. Lash kept bellowing "Wake up!" and running after me. Finally he ran out of wind and I disappeared from his view.

I drove to the campus coffee shop and had a cup of coffee. Then I drove back to the "Stud Farm." Lash was still out in front looking in both directions with a worried expression.

I parked and said, "Hi Lash!"

"Where have you been?" he asked.

"Coffee shop," I answered "Why?"

"How did you get there?" he asked.

"In my car." I answered.

"Oh" he said, "Do you remember driving there?"

"Sure," I said. Then I looked confused. "Wait a minute. I remember asking you to hypnotize me."

"Right!" he responded "And that's the _last_ time I'll ever hypnotize you."

That was exactly the reaction I wanted.

We all came up with untoward incidents like this. Gene Kalisz spontaneously became a Sheepeater one afternoon, started a fire in a coffee can, and sat wrapped in a blanket before it, chanting. We called Lash for help. He vowed never to hypnotize Kalisz again.

One afternoon Gene Taylor drank a lot of beer. When his bladder was full he went to Lash's room and asked to be hypnotized so he could remember everything he had to study for a test in his embryology course. Lash gladly complied. He put on his turban and had Gene lie on his bed. At this point, a group of us, in on the plot, showed up to watch the session. Lash loved an audience but pleaded for us to be silent.

As soon as a trance was induced, Gene, unable to restrain his bladder any longer, rolled over and, face down on Lash's bed, cut loose.

We onlookers, sitting on the floor could see the urine coming through the mattress and pooling under the bed. We convulsed with laughter while Lash pleaded for us to be silent and serious. He told Gene that he would instantly memorize every page he read in his embryology text and would confidently make an "A" on the next day's examination.

Then he ordered Gene to wake up. Gene did so and got out of Lash's bed. His jeans were soaked with urine. "What did you do to me?" Gene shrieked. "Right in front of my friends and classmates!"

"I'm so sorry," Lash stammered. "That hasn't happened before. I'm sorry Gene. I'll never hypnotize you again."

Soon Lash told me that he would never hypnotize another person again as long as he lived. Exactly the response we hoped for, and we did it without making him feel like a fool.

Towards the end of the school year it was time to give up on the practical jokes. John had lost his love for Nancy and lost interest in ever going again to Laramie, Lash had given up hypnotism- while awed by his power, he was afraid to use it. We felt we'd done enough in the name of entertainment. It was time to grow up.

Springtime! In a Western agricultural school like Colorado A&M University, that means rodeo time. At this time, our school became number one with our Intercollegiate National Champion Rodeo team. In fact, I met my wife at a college rodeo. She was the top barrel racer on our champion team and I won the team roping together with my classmate, Robroy Patterson. But that was the following year. This particular year, Lash had decided to enter the Whiskerino contest.

This was the era of short-hair.. Crewcuts were in vogue, as were clean-shaven faces. But, for the school rodeo, whoever grew the most luxurious beard would win the Whiskerino contest. Lash quit shaving.

After a few weeks he had a pitiful tuft of hair on his chin.

A group of us veterinary students were studying together when Lash came in.

"Sorry to bother you," he said "But is there anything that will stimulate hair growth?"

We all immediately seized upon the opportunity. "Sure," I said. "We have some stuff in the school hospital pharmacy we use to increase hair growth in show cattle. Why do you ask?"

"Is it safe for use in humans?"

Mike answered, "As a matter of fact, it was originally a human drug. It wasn't popular because it caused excessive hair growth."

"Right," said Gene Taylor. "It's called Hairsuit!"

"Can you get me some?" asked Lash.

"Why?" We asked.

"Aah! It's this beard. It's going nowhere!"

Val Farrel looked at me. "He deserves a good beard! Let's go down to the pharmacy and get him some."

Val and I went to the school pharmacy at 11pm We filled an ointment tin with a depilatory cream used to prepare rabbits for surgery. Rabbit skin is so delicate that rather than shaving the abdominal skin prior to surgery, a human depilatory cream is used instead. We labeled the tin "Hairsuit. To stimulate hair growth apply, leave on 20 minutes and then rinse off thoroughly." Then we mixed in some methylene blue dye.

The next day, everybody at the "Stud Farm" knew what was going to happen. We held a country music jam session in my room. It was a former foaling stall and the largest room on the place, housing three students. Gene Kalisz and Gene Taylor brought their guitars, I had my harmonica, and two other boys played their fiddles.

While the music played, Lash smeared the "Hairsuit" all over his face. Not everybody had a watch back then, and he kept asking when the 20 minutes were up. Then one student said, "Oh my gosh! It's been *40* minutes!"

Lash ran to the sink, (the only sink in the entire barn) and washed the cream off of his face. Of course, his beard came off with it and the guy with the watch said "Gee, I'm sorry. I read the watch wrong."

The next day Lash came to see us.

"I realize that you guys pulled a practical joke on me, and it didn't matter because my beard was a failure anyway."

Then, his voice broke and tears welled up in his eyes. "But I can't go through life without a beard. Is there an antidote for that stuff?"

Gene Taylor frowned sympathetically, looked at me and said, "He deserves an antidote. He's a good kid."

"Right!" I agreed.

We both hiked across to the campus and all the way to the vet school pharmacy. There we prepared a solution of silver nitrate.

Silver nitrate solution, if applied to the skin, will turn

it black once exposed to sunlight. It's even more effective at discoloring fingernails. We labeled it, "To restore hair growth, apply like shaving lotion to the skin every 15 minutes."

The next day was Saturday. A bunch of us went to town to the Dew Drop Inn. The University was in a dry county. Only 3.2% beer could be sold and the Dew Drop Inn was a beer parlor. We invited Lash to accompany us and once there, , we gave him the silver nitrate solution.

While we veterinary students drank beer, Lash dutifully applied the lotion to his face, which was now blue.

Finally, hours later, we all left and marched home. It was a brilliant, sunny fall day but Lash's face didn't blacken. It was still blue. Apparently our silver nitrate solution was too weak.

However, halfway home, Lash cried out "Hey! My nails are all black!"

"Oh, no!" I shuddered. "Paronychia pigmentosa!"

The other men all recoiled in horror. One shouted "Paronychia pigmentosa! The first sign of Rocky Mountain Leprosy!"

Lash squinted and looked at us sideways. "You guys! You must think I'm *gullible*!"

My hat! My new hat!

Chapter 8
Postgraduate Cowboy Humor

In 1956 I graduated with my D.V.M. degree. I went back to Arizona to work for other veterinarians and to marry Debby, the girl I'd met during my senior year in school.

I was kept far too busy to even think of practical jokes, but in 1957 we moved to California hoping to find or to create a group practice, which would allow for time off from a 24/7 profession.

The first year in California I worked for Dr. Ralph Reese of the Double R Veterinary Hospital in Calabasas. It was a mixed practice treating large and small animals in what was then a rural area. Our patients included livestock, horses, and house pets including several show dog kennels. One of the kennels was a renowned Basset Hound breeder and the owner, Paul, had become a good friend of Dr. Reese.

One rainy January day the staff of the Double R had nothing to do. Dr. Reese, who loved treating cattle and told me once that he guessed he was, "A cowboy at heart," got an idea. He suggested I call Paul, and in an affected Mexican accent, complain that the Basset Hounds were killing my sheep. There was a large flock of sheep near the kennel, herded by Hispanic shepherds.

I did it. I phoned Paul and said "Sir, I got the sheep behind your place and your dogs is killing my sheep."

Paul was outraged. "What? My dogs never leave these premises. That's impossible!"

"Please, sir," I said "I not mad. I know dogs do that. I only ask you keep your dogs in so my sheep don't die."

Paul raged, "My dogs can't kill sheep. You don't know what you're talking about."

"Look," I said "I not looking for you to pay. I just ask you keep your dogs away. I here at a vet with one of my dead sheep and he say one of those Bastard Hounds, those stupid looking dogs with long ears and little short feet kill this sheep. He can tell."

Paul was enraged. "Where are you? What vet told you that?"

"I at Double R. Doctor Reese cutting up my dead sheep and he say Bastard Hound did it."

At this Paul said, "Stay there! I'm on my way down."

I told our staff, "He's mad and he's coming down. What should we do?"

Our kennel boy, Barry, a future veterinarian, said, "Let me

get in the x-ray developing room. Tell him I went nuts, got violent, and you had to lock me in."

About ten minutes later ,Paul swerved into our parking lot, stormed in, and demanded of Dr. Reese, "What's going on here?"

We explained that the sheep man had suddenly flipped out, become violent, and that we had to lock him up in the x-ray developing room. At this point ,Barry started to hammer on the door, screaming "Let me out! Let me out!"

Paul said, "I'm calling the police!"

We realized that it was time to call a halt to the prank. We opened the door and let Barry out.

"Where is he?" thundered Paul.

"It's a joke," Dr. Reese said "We had nothing to do."

"No, I talked to him! Where is he?"

"It was me," I explained. Then, in my best Mexican accent I added "I so sorry I make you mad. I got no sheep. I just make joke."

Paul was silent for a long time. Then, apparently not yet having overcome his anger and still not fully realizing that he'd been the victim of a practical joke, he said "He blamed my dogs! My dogs couldn't kill his sheep."

Paul got revenge some time later. It was when the Russians made the first successful moon landing, putting Sputnik on the moon. I was on duty at the hospital after dark. Paul drove up and said "Have you heard what the Soviets did?"

I said "Yes. It's been on the radio all day."

"Did you see what they did to the moon?"

"What?" I asked, confused.

"Come outside and look at the moon"

I stepped outside. A huge full moon, glowing red, had just come over the horizon.

"What?" I said "What about the moon?"

Paul sneered "Those Communist bastards! They painted it red!"

Touché!

The Double R Veterinary Hospital was in Los Angeles County. Dead dogs were put into a freezer outside the hospital, unless the owner wanted to bury them at home or take them to a pet cemetery. The county regularly picked up the dead dogs in the freezer.

Debby and I had moved to the then-small town of Thousand Oaks, 15 miles from Dr. Reese's practice. Thousand Oaks was at the epicenter of ranching in the Conejo Valley. The only industry in the valley was a private zoo which served the movie and television industry when they needed wild animals. The zoo had a large number of big cats: lions, tigers, leopards, etc. To feed them, the zoo would pick up dead livestock from the ranches free of charge. The carcasses would be processed in a zoo butcher shop and the meat fed to the cats.

Once in a while a catastrophe had occurred. A cow or horse that had been euthanized by a veterinarian with an overdose of barbiturate anesthetic mistakenly found its way into the butcher shop. The meat was fed to the cats and the anesthetic contaminated meat caused toxicity. This ranged from dizziness, and stupor, to, occasionally, to the death of an animal.

A dog had died at the Double R, and unbeknownst to Dr. Reese, Barry and another teenaged future vet, Steve, decided to play a trick on me. They drove the body to Thousand Oaks at night, and laid it on my doorstep.

When I discovered it the next morning, I assumed that an inconsiderate resident of the little town, learning that a vet lived there,, had simply left a dead dog for me to deal with.

I took the body with me to the hospital and put it in the

freezer where it belonged. Later that morning, Barry and Steve mischievously asked if I had any surprises at home. Once I realized that I had been the victim of an ill-conceived prank, I planned my revenge.

"You mean that dog I found outside my door came from here?"

They both nodded, grinning.

Then I pretended shock. "Oh, no! I thought it was a natural death so I dropped it off at the zoo to feed to the big cats."

I satisfactorily noted their alarm.

"I'd better call and warn them not to butcher that dog. It was put to sleep with barbiturates."

I phoned my wife and pretended to be talking to the zoo. Then I sadly hung up and said "It's too late! They fed the dog to a leopard. I'll go see it on my way home tonight."

The next morning the boys anxiously asked how the leopard was. I replied "Deep anesthesia. I get no reflexes. I've got it on I.V. fluids and supportive therapy and I'll see it again tonight."

This went on for a week. Then, finally, when I came into the hospital I shook my head. "The leopard died. Just too much barbiturate. I tried. They're really mad. They don't blame me because they know that some unknown person put that dog on my doorstep, but they're determined to find out who it was and are going to prosecute them."

Both Steve and Barry made it into vet school and 41 years later I met Steve's mother. She told me that he was a successful practitioner and then added, "You know, he's never gotten over his guilt for being responsible for that leopard's death."

I told her the truth and suggested that she tell her son to relieve him of that long-held guilt trip. Haven't heard from him so I don't know if she told him, or if he's carefully plotting his revenge.

"Watch that badger hole," Tom!

Chapter 9
Alumni Pranks

Yes, Walter Cole was the veterinary student mentioned in an earlier chapter who, when 'hypnotized' by John, morphed into a Paleolithic caveman. Like me, Walter started his practice in Tucson, Arizona, and remained there for the rest of his life.

After one year of practice in Tucson, I went to California with my bride, Debby, seeking a group practice.

Twenty-five years later, I received a letter from a woman in Tucson. There was no return address but I knew from the postmark that the letter had been mailed in Tucson. The letter went as follows, in a shaky penciled handwriting:

"Dear Dr. Miller,

I am sure you remember Snippy. When I first brought him to you fourteen years ago he fit in your hand. He was only seven week old. Well, Snippy is old now, and we moved to Tucson years ago which is why you haven't seen us for a long time.

Well, the vet here says that Snippy has old age kidney disease. He has been on a special diet but is worse now and the doctor says there is nothing more that he can do.

I know what a wonderful vet you are and how much you liked Snippy. I am sure that you can help him. So, I am shipping him to you and when he is well you can ship him back to me and please include a bill so I can pay you."

There was no signature and I immediately wondered if this could be a practical joke. Who did I know in Tucson who could pull a prank like this, designed to agitate me?

Why, Walter Cole, of course.

Assuming, with some doubt, that Doctor Cole was behind this improbable letter, I dismissed the whole thing from my mind.

Not long after, I received a message from the railroad station in Oxnard, thirty miles away.

"Doctor Robert Miller. There's a cage here with a dog in it. Please come and pick it up as soon as possible."

Disturbed and rather upset, I drove to Oxnard to find a cage with a life sized toy dog in it and a sign on the cage which said, "Gotcha!" It was signed "Walter."

Several months later I drove to Tucson with my family to visit my ageing parents for Thanksgiving.

As we drove east I said to my wife, "You know, while we're in Tucson we ought to pull a prank on Walter Cole. I owe him one."

Debby agreed. Great! But what can we do?"

My thirteen-year-old daughter, Laurel, piped up: "Why don't I go in with Molly and say that I want my puppy vaccinated. Doctor Cole won't know me and I'll tell him to send my father a bill for the vaccination."

Molly, our 13-year-old Australian Shepherd, was with us on the trip.

Knowing my daughter, a ranch-raised teen with a reverence for cowboy humor, I agreed.

We arrived at my parents' home, and I telephoned Walter's office. I told the receptionist who I was and explained that I planned to pull a practical joke on her boss.

"Oh, good!" she said.

So we set an appointment for a puppy vaccination.

At the appointed hour, Laurel, sloppily dressed and chewing bubble gum, was shown into an examination room.

Debby and I came into the crowded waiting room and stationed ourselves on either side of the exam room door. The following conversation between Doctor Cole and Laurel ensued:

"Good morning young lady. What can we do for you?"

"Well, this homeless man gave us this puppy and we want it vaccinated."

"I see. Well let's lift her up on the table and we'll take a look at her." (Grunts)

Then, after a pause:

"First of all, this isn't a puppy. This is an older dog."

"Nah-uh! The man said!"

"(Laughs)" No, really, this is a mature dog. See those yellow teeth? A pup's teeth would be white."

"Yeah! My dad has teeth like that."

Debby and I are stifling laughter outside the door.

"Are you here by yourself? Where are your parents?"

"My dad's across the street at the bar (It was 9:15 a.m.).

"Can you go get him, so I can talk to him?"

"Naw! Once he starts drinking beer, he won't quit."

(Again, Debby and I are convulsing at this unrehearsed dialogue.)

"Well, how about your Mom? Is she around?"

"Naw! She ran off with my teacher a few weeks ago."

"I aaah, see. Just a moment, I need to go out and speak to my receptionist."

Walter comes out and sees us. He startles.

"Oh! Look who's here!"

Then, as realization hits him in the crowded waiting room, he shouts

"You S.O.B.! You got me!"

Yes, we did, and revenge is sweet.

Calvin nearly died laughing last night, before they turned in, when he heard about how Spencer had freaked out at finding a snake in his boot.

Chapter 10
Practice Years

A most imaginative and effective practical joke was played upon me in 1971. Grant Gerson owned Calamigos Ranch in the Santa Monica Mountains. The first ranch call I made after I moved to California in 1957 was to the ranch to see Grant's stallion, Prince.

Grant, forever in cowboy boots and a Western hat, was a jovial, upbeat, friendly person and he became a friend, as well as a loyal client.

In 1971, I was in Kitzbuhl, Austria, attending a meeting of the Sierra Veterinary Medical Association (SVMA), a group I founded in 1960. We met every winter at a different ski resort to enjoy a week of C.E. (continuing education) and skiing. This was the first meeting held in Europe, and several European colleagues had joined us.

I came into the lobby of our hotel one afternoon for the evening lectures, after a day of skiing. A group of my colleagues stood near the front desk and as I entered, they pointed at me and said to the hotel manager, "There he is. That's him. That's Doctor

Miller."

I looked up as the manager said "Doctor Miller? A telephone call for you from America."

When you're overseas and receive a phone call from home, you're immediately concerned. Something must be wrong.

I took the phone apprehensively and said, "Hello?" The following conversation ensued:

"Bob? This is Grant."

"Grant? Grant Gerson?"

"Yes! Glad I could reach you. Prince has been off feed. He doesn't act right. Can you come see him?"

"Grant" I responded. "Do you know where I am?"

"Yes! In Kitzbuhl, Austria. They told me. Can you come see Prince?"

I was speechless. But by 1971 I had two associates.

"Grant," I said "I'm in *Austria*. Call the clinic and Doctor Kind or Doctor Rich can see him."

"But, Bob, you know him best. You could fly home tonight and see him tomorrow, and then fly back to Austria the next night. Prince really needs you to see him."

I had always been impressed with Grant's logical mind and

his common sense, but this was nuts. I had either overestimated his sanity or perhaps he'd suffered a mental breakdown.

"Grant! I'm more than six-thousand miles away. I'm at a veterinary meeting. I have to do a lecture. I can't leave here."

"But Prince needs you. Bob! You have to see him."

My mind whirled in confusion, and again I tried to explain how unreasonable Grant was being. And then, I remembered a conversation we'd once had, wherein both of us had agreed that our favorite pastimes were riding horses and skiing. Hey! Wait a minute! He's a skier!

"Grant," I said. "Where are you calling from?"

"Kitzbuhl," he responded.

It seems that Grant had gone up a chairlift with another American. Then he learned that the American was a veterinarian attending a professional meeting.

Grant said "You're a vet? I wonder if you know my vet. His name is Bob Miller and he lives in Thousand Oaks, California."

"He's here!" the skier replied. "He's at our meeting here in Kitzbuhl."

Grant was delighted. "Don't tell him I'm here, too," he said. "I'm going to have some fun with him."

Dr. Warren Walker is a long-time friend and colleague. He's also an ex-cowboy and appreciates practical jokes. Once we attended another veterinary meeting together at a ski resort. As we unloaded our luggage from the shuttle, a man came out of the lobby to greet us. He was obviously a staff member so Warren asked him if he could help bring his baggage into the hotel. The man answered, "I'm not a bellman. I'm the hotel manager."

"Good," said Warren with a straight face. "That means I won't have to tip you." Thus began a friendly, humorous feud.

One day it stormed so badly the ski lifts were closed. So, after the morning lecture we all repaired to the lobby to spend the day fraternizing. When we got to the lobby a life size dummy was hanging from the rafters by a rope around its neck. A sign on its chest read "Doctor Walker."

But, revenge is sweet, and Park City, Utah, was a very small town. The village policemen are well-known.

The next day two officers showed up and arrested Warren.

Despite his protests, a demand for an explanation, and his insistence on telephoning his lawyer, the officers offered no explanation. The town actually had a modern jail, but it also had a

19th century frontier jail and not until the police took Warren there and chained him to a wall did he realize that it was all a practical joke.

At that same meeting, Dr. Vincent Jessup, a cattle practitioner and the son of a prominent California family of cattlemen, became a victim. We were all at dinner after the evening lecture when one of our group announced he had a ski parka to auction off. Not until the bids were well over the original cost of the parka did Vince realize that he was bidding for his own article of clothing.

Eunice Larson is an M.D. I got to know her because she did the pathology for the Los Angeles Zoo, and since I did a lot of zoo animal practice I needed someone experienced in those species to do my pathology. Over many years Eunice became a personal friend.

Nobody ever showed up uninvited to our home, , because we were too far out in the country. So, when Eunice decided to bring a grown nephew out to visit us and see our ranch, we decided to have some fun.

My wife, Debby, had borrowed an amazingly realistic chimpanzee costume for Halloween from one of our clients. This client was one of several in our practice who supplied zoo animals to the movie and television industry in Hollywood. His farm is just up the canyon from our place. The costume was used for certain scenes when a real chimp couldn't do the desired scene. As I said, it was very realistic and the wearer, who had to be petite in size, couldn't see clearly because there were only two tiny pinholes to look through, in the center of the very life-like eyes.

Our plan was to have Eunice send her nephew to our front door and ring the bell. She had already told him that I treated all kinds of zoo animals. When the bell rang I planned to hammer on the door, hooting like a chimpanzee. I can do this so realistically that it fools real chimps. Then, after an appropriate pause, I was to hide behind the door, swing it open and there would be my wife, in the chimp suit, bouncing up and down right in front of the door.

Half an hour before their arrival, Debby got into the costume.

When I heard a car coming up our road, I told Debby, "Quick, get by the front door," and then I hid behind it. I heard the car's engine stop, and our front gate open. Then, the doorbell rang.

I immediately started slamming both fists against the door, and while Debby bounced up and down on all fours, I screamed and hooted for about half a minute. Then I swung the door open.

Peeking through the space between the door and the frame I saw two white faced open-mouthed young men. They were wearing suits and ties and their eyes bulged.

They were Jehovah's Witnesses. Debby, unable to see them, kept bouncing up and down.

Realizing that a terrible mistake had been made, I stepped out from behind the door and said "Good morning. May I help you?"

The pharmaceutical companies sent us vaccines refrigerated with ice bags. But one company used cans of frozen orange soda Thus, we always had cans of soda in our refrigerator.

One day, Arthur, our intern, was late to work. So, I opened a can of orange soda, and poured some into a urinometer, the glass tubular flask used for urinalysis. Then, I stationed myself at the microscope and, when Arthur came in, I waved at the urinometer and said, "Art, run a UA on that specimen, will you?"

So, while I pretended to be busy looking through the microscope, Arthur went to work. After a while I heard him say, "Holy cow! A four plus sugar. I got a very high sugar!"

I slapped my forehead and said, "Oh! Of course! *Diabetes*! It should have been obvious! Polydipsia! Polyuria! Weight loss! The dog has diabetes! It should have been obvious. I must be getting old! Good thing I ran a urinalysis!"

Arthur responded, "I'm going to check it for ketones."

While he busied himself preparing to run another test, I pulled the vial of "urine" closer to me, stuck a finger in it and then stuck the finger in my mouth.

"Oh, gosh," I said "It's *loaded* with sugar! Taste that, Art."

Arthur, who'd watched me with a surprised sideways glance, said "No thanks! I'll just use my little chemicals here."

I pretended surprise, "Why, Art! Are you squeamish? Do you know why we call one disease "Diabetes Insipidus" and another disease "Diabetes Mellitus?"

"Yes, I know," said Arthur. "Insipidus means 'tasteless' and 'Mellitus' means 'sweet.' I know that. And I know that long ago doctors, including physicians, had to taste the patients' urine in order to differentiate, but, if you don't mind. I'll just use my little laboratory here."

"Well, I sneered.. "Aren't *you* particular?" And, with that I picked up the urinometer full of soda and chugged the entire thing.

Arthur retched, and then, suddenly, he realized what was happening and it turned into convulsive laughter.

It should now be apparent that it's easy to lure veterinarians into succumbing to a practical joke. There was a ranch in Agoura that had a bison in one pasture together with a bunch of cattle. One day, I noticed it lying close to the fence along the highway, upright, with its nose pressed to the ground. I thought it was just in an unusual position, but several days later it was obviously dead. It was August and the smell of the decomposing body was noticeable as far as a quarter of a mile away. We discussed it in our office and wondered why the carcass had not been buried, or carted away for rendering.

About six days after it had died I wrote on Dr. Larry Dresher's schedule, "Necropsy buffalo along highway in Agoura. Submit tissues including brain to Los Angeles County Veterinary Laboratory. They request this be done today."

Larry came in, looked at his schedule and said "Holy mackerel! Why didn't they request this before the thing got so badly decomposed. And they want brain tissue. I'm going to have to open the skull. Oh, what a nasty job! Well I'd better get out there now while it's cool. It's going to top a hundred degrees today."

Mercifully we told him he didn't have to go. It was just a joke. <u>But,</u> he was ready to go. That's the significant point of this story.

I mentioned earlier how easily veterinarians can be duped into falling for a practical joke.

A rhinoceros, even if born in captivity, is still very aggressive and dangerous. One day, arriving at the hospital early, I looked at the daily schedule. One of my partners, Bob Kind, was on surgery, but all that he had scheduled was one tomcat to neuter. So I added this: "Dehorn rhinoceros."

When Bob arrived he looked at the schedule.

"Is the rhinoceros coming here?" he asked. "No," I explained. "They measured him and he won't fit through the door. You'll have to go over to Jungleland and do it there." The

Jungleland zoo was only a couple of hundred yards from our clinic

"Why are they dehorning him?" asked Bob.

"Because he's so nasty. He's hurt several people. Also, they say they can get more money for the horn in China than the animal is worth."

Bob mumbled to himself and left the room. He returned several minutes later and said, "I know that horn has a boney core so I guess I can cut through the bone with a Gigli wire surgical saw."

"Bob" I said. "It's a joke. You don't have to dehorn a rhinoceros."

"Well," said Bob, obviously relieved, "I had to see an elephant recently with a broken tusk, so why not a rhino that needs dehorning?"

Chapter 11
Inspirational Practical Jokes

During the late sixties a veterinary conference was held at the University of California, Santa Cruz campus in Northern California.

Located in the midst of redwood forest, it's the most beautiful campus I've seen.

Now, this was the late sixties. We doctors of veterinary medicine attended in the proper attire for that time; suits and ties. But the students dressed differently. This was the Hippie Era. Long-haired students lounged under the trees, playing flutes and guitars. Young women wore flowers in their hair, long dresses, and bare feet. Keep in mind, too, that campus demonstrations and riots were common at the time.

During the lunch break the vets retreated to an elevated restaurant – a sort of tree house cafeteria. As we ate, we read the campus newspaper, rich in profound political and social opinions.

I remember that it was at that lunch that I first discovered carrot cake. The name of the dessert intrigued me and I thought it was delicious.

Grouped at one of the tables we men of a previous generation came up with an inspirational plot.

We decided to publish a fraudulent copy of the school newspaper, and distribute it on April First.

The headline would read "Weyerhauser Lumber Company donates millions to U.C. Santa Cruz."

Below the headline was an explanation: The huge lumber company was making the monetary contribution to the school providing that a Department of Forestry would be established, and that over the years all of the redwood trees on campus would be harvested.

Then, to farther enrage the students, a second article explained that an Animal Science Department would be simultaneously created, paid for by the Armour company so that the campus could be grazed by cattle once the trees were removed. Then, after the cattle were mature enough, they would be moved to a feedlot, also on campus, for finishing before being slaughtered at a campus packing plant. The meat would then be served in the university cafeteria.

One of the colleagues attending was a faculty member at Stanford University and was certain that he could get that school's newspaper to print our proposed counterfeit Santa Cruz publication.

We all enthusiastically agreed to come on April first to the U.C. Santa Cruz campus to witness the hysteria, and to discourage any destruction of the administration building by rioting mobs.

Then, after the conference, we all went home to our busy practices and nothing ever came of our plan.

After I retired from practice and began an unplanned but full-time second career teaching horse behavior, I was invited to Argentina for a month to do seminars throughout the country. My hosts were, ranchers Gloria and Malcolm Cook, native Argentines who speak perfect English. As a result of this trip, my wife and I have become good friends with the Cooks, and, following a seminar I had to do in Hawaii, we invited them to do a tour of the islands. They agreed and we arranged to meet at the airport on Maui.

A colleague and long-time friend, Dr. Ian Coster and his wife Pat, accompanied us on the flight to Maui. We told them that we were going to meet friends from Argentina at the airport, and that the six of us would travel together to our destination hotel, which was about a half hour's bus ride from the airport.

Ian loves to learn foreign languages. He's fluent in French, and knows a smattering of several other tongues, including Spanish.

So, when the Cooks arrived, I was inspired, when I greeted them, to say "Pretend that you don't speak English. My friend loves to try to speak Spanish, and we'll have some fun."

After introductions we boarded the shuttle.. Pat Coster and Gloria Cook sat together. Gloria pretended to speak broken English. "Me no English speak. You Miller friend? We go Hawaii. We see." Pat responded, "Good! Good! Bueno. Me no speak mucho Spanish. Español. No speak."

Debby and I sat together behind them and, behind us sat Malcolm and Ian. We listened gleefully to the conversation. Malcolm pretended to speak not one word of English.

"Estoy ranchero. Vacas y caballos. (I am a rancher. Cattle and horses).

Ian responded. "Me too. Tengo rancho. Me veterinario. Yo soy un veterinario. Tengo rancho con caballos. Horses. You understand? Comprende?"

"Si! Yo comprendo!"

All the way to the hotel these conversations went on, much to our delight. Finally, as we neared our destination I turned around to face Ian and Malcolm.

"How are you guys getting along?" I asked.

"Oh, great" Ian answered. "A little English. A little Spanish. A lot of sign language. We just made a bet. I bet Malcolm a case of beer that at the end of the week I'll speak better Spanish than he does English. We're going to teach each other all week. But *I'm* going to win because I already know some Spanish and *he* can't speak a word of English."

Malcolm looked arrogantly at his companion and said, in a very British accent, "But you have already *lost* old boy!"

Ian was dumbfounded. Then he looked at me and spoke. I can't repeat his words here, but they were in English.

We had an internship program in our group practice for twenty five years. The candidates included men and women who had just obtained their doctorates, and we intentionally sought alumni from various schools both in America and abroad.

Every intern, of course, received a goldmine of information from our experienced staff, but we also learned from them.

Without exception, each intern shared with us something new that they'd learned in school.

There were, of course, many inevitable amusing incidents with each internship. For example, one Sunday when I was on large animal emergency duty, I went into our animal hospital to pick up some supplies. Our intern, Dr. Simmons, was on small animal emergency duty wearing shorts and a T-shirt. After he dismissed the patient, I reprimanded him. I said, "Bob, you know that we have a dress code here in the hospital. The doctors are supposed to wear a business shirt, tie, and smock."

"Oh, sure" he said. "But its Sunday and the clients will realize that I came from home to take care of their animals on an emergency basis."

"No matter," I replied. "Even on emergencies we dress professionally. Do you know why?"

"No," he said.

"Here in Southern California," I explained, "we have a very diverse clientele. Ranchers and cowboys, high-tech engineers, and gardeners. It varies from hippies to affluent retired couples. So, if you are sloppily dressed, it will cause some clients to disrespect you, but if you are properly attired, all of the clients will accept that. Do you know why that is?"

"Because the older folks are narrow-minded and intolerant?" he asked.

"No! It's because everybody, regardless of their background, wants a doctor to be a serious person, whether the patient is a human or an animal. They want a serious doctor."

"I see," Bob said. "I'll remember that. Makes sense."

"There's another reason you should never to see a patient wearing shorts."

"Oh? What's that?"

"Well, it hasn't happened yet, but it will! While you're talking to the owner, the dog will pee on your leg. You don't want to be wearing shorts."

We had one intern from Sweden. One day, I had to see a horse at the Paramount Pictures Western movie set.

The set, where countless films had been made, had a Main Street with the usual hitching posts, saloons, mercantile, a barber shop, etc.

Karl was immediately entranced by the location. He took

out his camera and started shooting pictures while I dealt with the lone horse and its owner. I let Karl keep on taking pictures.

Finally, when we were ready to leave, Karl said "Why are there no people here? Why is the town so empty?"

I explained, "Because they aren't making a movie right now."

Realization flooded his face. This was a movie set, not a real town.

Sabina was a new graduate from Germany. She applied for our internship and we accepted her. This alarmed her father, who was also a veterinarian, as was her brother. Her father pleaded, "America is so dangerous. I see so much killing on TV and in American movies. I fear that I will never see you again." Nevertheless, Sabina accepted our internship and we remain friends to this very day.

She purchased a Western hat and wore it when we made ranch calls. One day, we passed a herd of Texas longhorn cattle. "Oh," she exclaimed. "Can we stop so I can take some pictures to send home?"

"Sure," I said. "Why don't you crawl through the fence and pose with them and I'll take the photo. They're gentle. I know them. They're my patients."

She did so, and I handed her a lariat. "Here! Pretend you're going to rope one."

She sent the picture home and it elicited a desperate response from her father, who pleaded for her to come home because she was obviously in the "Wild West" and he feared for her survival.

Rick was one of our interns from the University of California veterinary school at Davis, California. One day he decided to play a joke on me. A grateful client had presented our staff with a big can of Almond Roca, those delicious little chocolate bars studded with crushed almonds and wrapped in gold foil.

We were scheduled to have a staff meeting the next morning. As Chief of Staff, my seat was at the head of a long table. Doctor Rick noticed that the confections looked remarkably like a cat stool with particles of sand attached from a litter box. So, he took a cat stool from a sandbox in one of the cages, wrapped it in gold foil, and placed it on the table in front of my seat. Then he put a real Almond Roca on the table in front of all the other chairs.

Then, Rick told all the other doctors - we had ten by this time – what he'd done. The word went around the hospital, and soon everybody but me knew what was going to happen when I opened the foil and tried to eat the candy.

But, one of our assistants was apparently looking for a raise, because he told me of the plot. I thanked him and, late at night, I went back to the meeting room in the hospital, discarded the fake candy, and put a real Almond Roca in its place.

Next morning, at the meeting, there was an air of expectancy. Midway through the agenda, I picked up the candy and held it. When I spoke I gestured with that hand. Every eye followed my hand. Dr. Kind sat rigidly, his lips tightly closed. Dr. Peddie's eyes gleamed. Dr. Dresher's head turned away so I couldn't see his suppressed laughter. Dr. Rick turned red, trying to conceal his anticipation. Another doctor hunched over studying the table but, his eyes were turned towards me.

Then, I casually undid the foil wrapper, exposing the encrusted brown morsel within. I held it in my palm, gesturing from time to time. The suspense was audible in the room.

Then, suddenly, with never having actually touched the candy, I popped it into my mouth.

Everyone in the room gasped, and intern Rick screamed, "No, no!"

I chewed methodically, looked around at everybody, and said "What? What's the problem?

Then, I looked at Rick and said, "A degree from U.C. Davis, even when combined with treachery and cunning, is no match for experience."

We brought our mare to breed to your stud.

Chapter 12
A Half Century Long Practical Joke

I mentioned Rex Hinshaw earlier. He's older than me and graduated from the Colorado vet school in 1952. He was involved in what is probably the longest practical joke in history, to the best of my knowledge. It went on for half a century.

Rex is now retired a doctor of veterinary medicine who spent his career in Prescott, Arizona. But, he was a cowboy and cattle rancher throughout his life.

Doctor Farquarson was a deeply respected and somewhat feared elder professor at the Colorado veterinary school. He had a propensity for calling out a student's name and demanding an answer to a question. One day he said "Mister Kavanaugh!" There was nobody in the class named Kavanaugh. He called the name out again, demandingly, while the class looked about in confusion. Kavanaugh seemed to be absent.

Later, members of the class discovered that a Kavanaugh had been in Dr. Farquarson's class several years earlier.

The incident became a class joke, and when they graduated, they took a traditional class photograph. Beneath it all the students' names were listed. In the top row of the picture, there are ten students. But, eleven names are listed. The last is "Norvil O. Kavanaugh." That's N.O. Kavanaugh. No Kavanaugh, get it?

This was the beginning of a half-century-long practical joke, played by a class upon their alma mater.

For 50 years, Norvil Kavanaugh made annual contributions to Colorado State University. At major veterinary conventions there are usually alumni meetings, and a dean or important faculty member in attendance. Members of the class of 1952, when they signed in at such events, added the name Norvil Kavanaugh.

His address was the same as a real classmate's- that of Dr. Rex Hinshaw, but nobody at the school seemed to have noticed that fact. Norvil regularly was sent correspondence, alumni newsletters, and the alumni magazine at the Hinshaw address. Kavanaugh also received the usual notification of alumni events and requests for donations to which he generously complied.

When the veterinary college at Colorado State University celebrated its centennial, Norvil Kavanaugh had been an alumnus for half of the school's history.

I was invited to be the keynote speaker at this event. Because I'm a cartoonist, they invited me to speak, anticipating an entertaining talk.

I telephoned Rex Hinshaw and asked if I could reveal the entire Kavanaugh story. Rex protested. "Oh, no! You'll spoil the joke."

"Rex" I responded. "It's gone on for over fifty years. It's a world record! Half of your class has passed on. Here's a chance for a final laugh. Reveal the truth in front of the faculty, administrators, and the rest of the alumni who weren't in your class."

Rex said, "Let me think about it." A couple of weeks later I received a reluctant answer in the mail. There was a copy of that graduation photo, a letter giving me permission to expose the whole story, and copies of letters sent to Kavanaugh over the years from the deans. Some of the letters said how pleased they were to see him. They expressed appreciation for his loyalty, and complimented him on his youthful and vigorous appearance. They hoped to see him again soon.

When I spoke at the reunion and told the story I had a projector with which I was able to display the graduation photo and letters from the deans.

The current dean and two previous deans were in the audience, and they nearly fell out of their chairs laughing.

In the annals of collegiate humor, the story of Norvil O.

Kavanaugh must hold the record for practical joke longevity. Given the cowboy upbringing of so many of the students of that era, I'm sure that its creativity owes a lot to the ranchhand propensity for practical jokes.

Amazingly, Dr. Norvil O. Kavanaugh is still a member of important veterinary medical associations. He still gets mail from his alma mater. Moreover, I've been told, his daughter, Nancy Kavanaugh, applied for admission to Colorado State University's College of Veterinary Medicine and Biomedical Sciences, but for some reason, was turned down. There is no Nancy Kavanaugh.

If there's a longer lasting practical joke than the one pulled by the Colorado veterinary class of 1952, I'd love to hear about it.

If I do hear about one, I'll bet some guy with a cowboy background thought it up.

This may not be a profitable business, but one must consider
the intangible benefits, such as the lifestyle one enjoys.

Wilbur, why don't you let someone else
handle the iron for a while?

Say, doctor, you don't happen to have some of that DMSO, do you, for my old horse up at the cow camp? He's got a sore back.

Other Works by Dr. Robert M. Miller

Books

Natural Horsemanship Explained - From Heart to Hands
The Revolution in Horsemanship - Co-authored with Rick Lamb
Understanding the Ancient Secrets of the Horse's Mind
Imprint Training of the Newborn Foal
Yes, We Treat Aardvarks
Mind Over Miller
Handling the Equine Patient - A Manual for Veterinary Students & Technicians

Equine Videos

Understanding Horses
Safer Horsemanship
Early Learning
Control of the Horse
Influencing the Horse's Mind
The Causes of Lameness

Cartoon Books

Am I Getting To Old For This?
The Second Oldest Profession
A Midstream Collection
Ranchin', Ropin' an' Doctorin' A book of cowboy and veterinary cartoons
Is It An Emergency? A Book of Dog Cartoons by RMM

Websites

www.robertmmiller.com
www.rmmcartoons.com

CPSIA information can be obtained
at www.ICGtesting.com
Printed in the USA
BVHW040528011221
622944BV00007B/130